KOREAN WAR HERO

SGT. RECKLESS
THE WAR HORSE

by Melissa Higgins   illustrated by Álvaro Iglesias

Content Consultant: Robin Hutton, founder
Operation Reckless, Sgt. Reckless Memorial Fund

PICTURE WINDOW BOOKS
a capstone imprint

Battle after battle, U.S. Marine Lieutenant Eric Pedersen watched his soldiers trudge through rice paddies and up steep hills. It was 1952. Fighting in the Korean War was fierce. Bullets whizzed over soldiers' heads as they hauled heavy ammo to roaring recoilless rifles. The soldiers' work was slow and hard.

Lieutenant Pedersen had a crazy idea. What his platoon needed was a packhorse—a brave packhorse—with the heart of a soldier.

Pedersen visited a racetrack in Seoul, South Korea, in October 1952. Inside the stable a small, reddish-brown filly caught his eye. Four-year-old Flame was healthy and confident. She seemed to trust Pedersen. She didn't shy away from him.

With $250, the sale was completed. Flame readily climbed into the trailer behind Pedersen's jeep.

It was just before dark when Pedersen and Flame got to camp. The Marines quickly took to the little red horse. They renamed her Reckless, after their recoilless guns.

The Marines had no horse feed when Reckless arrived, so they took her to the mess tent. Her first meal at camp was a loaf of bread and dry oatmeal. The following day Reckless gulped down scrambled eggs and coffee.

Eventually the Marines bought Reckless horse feed. But she always ate whatever the Marines offered her, including apples, carrots, and chocolate bars.

9

Before going to battle, Reckless completed basic training. Her boot camp (or "hoof camp") sergeant taught Reckless to step over wire. She learned to duck under enemy fire by lying down or kneeling.

Brave Reckless was willing to do anything she was asked. She just needed to look things over and trust who was giving her directions.

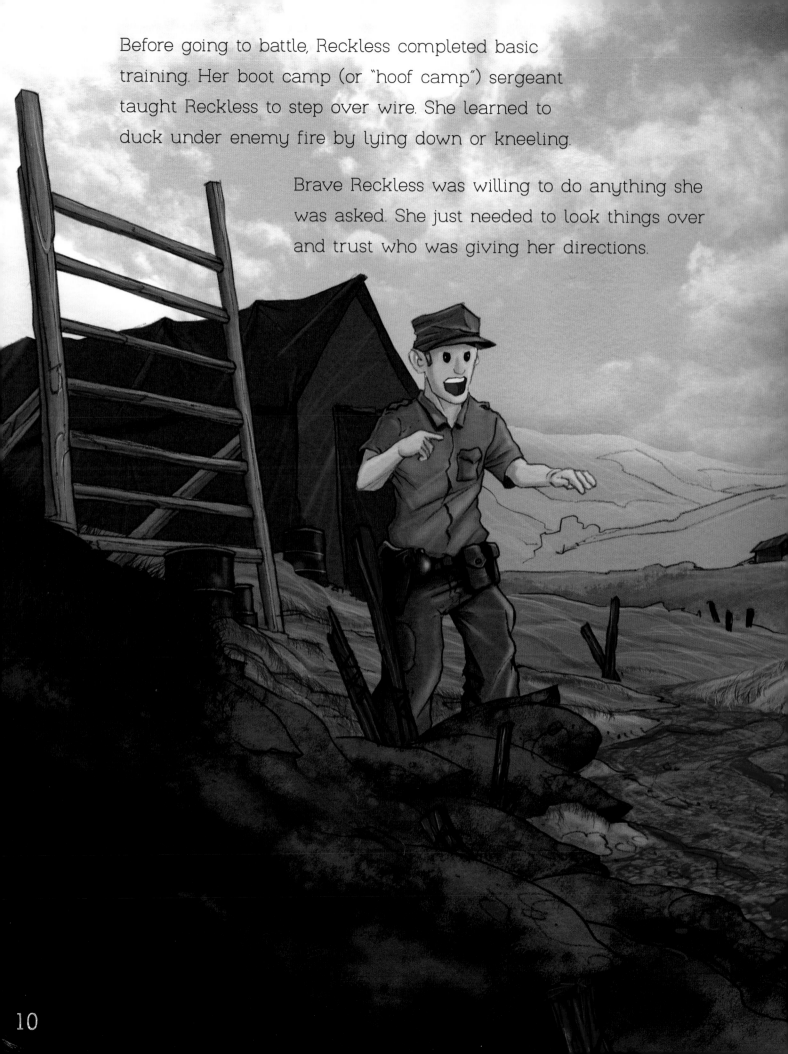

Finally Reckless was ready to be tested under fire. Would the loud noise and confusion of battle send her running away, like any normal horse?

As a soldier led Reckless toward the firing site, the recoilless rifle blasted. The shot roared across the hills. Reckless leapt high in the air. All four of her hooves left the ground.

Reckless landed, shaking with fear. Her handler spoke calmly to her. With each gun blast, Reckless shook less and less. She did not bolt. She was a true Marine.

In the following six months, Reckless proved herself in many battles. Following the sound of the recoilless gun, she often delivered ammo to the gun crew by herself. The gunners rewarded her with a piece of hard candy from their C-rations.

In the early morning of March 26, 1953, Reckless nervously paced. In the distance enemy gunfire pierced the darkness. Reckless and her unit would be joining a dangerous battle for a group of hills called the Nevada Complex.

Reckless' handler tried
to calm her as he loaded rounds
of heavy ammo onto her harness.
Her handler led her up the steep and twisting trail
to the first gun site. Gunfire blasted all around them,
but Reckless delivered the ammo.

Reckless made it to the site without bolting. Then hour after hour, load after load, Reckless took to the trails alongside her fellow Marines. On one trip, an explosion blasted nearby. A piece of shrapnel cut Reckless above her eye. A short time later, a piece of shrapnel cut her side. But she kept going, often heading out on her own. She made two trips to every Marine's station.

Reckless made 51 trips to different gun positions. She traveled more than 35 battle-torn miles (56 kilometers). She carried 386 rounds of ammo.

Finally, after 72 hours, the battle drew to a close. By supplying the ammo that helped end the battle, Reckless saved lives. She had worked as hard as any Marine. She earned the love and respect of the entire 1st Marine Division.

21

The fighting in the Korean War stopped in July 1953. No longer needed to haul ammo shells, Reckless traveled with her platoon. She helped string communication wire.

At night she visited Marines in their tents, especially
when it was cold outside. In addition to eating whatever
handouts the men shared, she also drank Coca-Cola.
She liked to drink out of a glass.

In honor of her bravery and service, Reckless was promoted to sergeant in 1954. She was later promoted again to the rank of staff sergeant.

Reckless was a true part of the team. When the platoon shipped out of Korea, the Marines refused to leave their four-legged sergeant behind.

SSgt. RECKLESS
5th MARINES
FIRST MARINE DIVISION

Sgt. Reckless arrived in San Francisco, California, on November 10, 1954. Old friends and reporters crowded around her. She had become famous.

Reckless lived at the Marine base at Camp Pendleton, near San Diego, California. She made guest appearances and joined her 5th Marines on 100-mile (161-km) marches.

27

Besides her two promotions, Reckless received many military decorations. These included two Purple Hearts, a Presidential Unit Citation with star, Good Conduct Medal, United Nations Service Medal, National Defense Service Medal, Korean Service Medal, Navy Unit Commendation, and Republic of Korea Presidential Unit Citation.

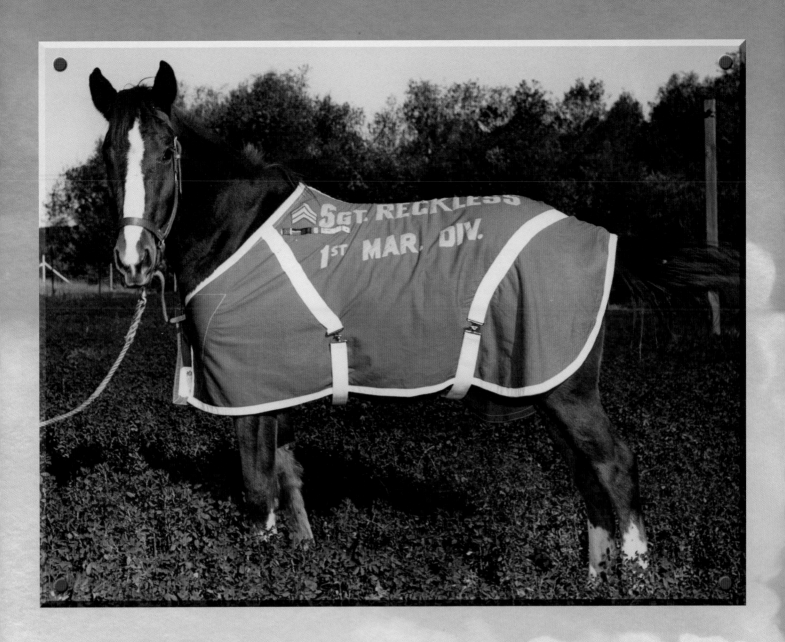

Reckless retired from her military service at Camp Pendleton. Over the years she gave birth to four foals. As she aged Reckless developed arthritis in her back. In 1968 she suffered from a fall in her pasture. While in surgery for her injuries, she quietly passed away.

Sixty years after the Korean War, Reckless' bravery and loyalty were not forgotten. On July 26, 2013, a life-size statue of Reckless was unveiled at the National Museum of the Marine Corps in Quantico, Virginia. Marines came from all over the country to honor the little red horse with the big heart.

GLOSSARY

ammo—bullets and other objects that can be fired from weapons; ammo is short for ammunition

decorations—military honors, such as medals

filly—a young female horse

handler—a person who trains or manages a horse for work or military duty

lieutenant—a rank in the U.S. military above sergeant and below captain

mess tent—a place where soldiers eat

platoon—a group of soldiers that work together; a platoon is commanded by a lieutenant

promote—to give a higher rank in the military

recoilless—without a kickback

shrapnel—pieces that have broken off from an explosive shell

unit—a group of soldiers

READ MORE

Andrekson, Judy. *Gunner: Hurricane Horse.* Plattsburgh, N.Y.: Tundra Books of Northern New York, 2010.

Cantrell, Charlie, and Dr. Rachel Wagner. *A Friend for Einstein, the Smallest Stallion.* New York: Disney-Hyperion, 2011.

Petty, Kate. *Horse Heroes: True Stories of Amazing Horses.* DK Readers. New York: DK Publishing, 2012.

BEYOND THE STORY

After "hoof" camp, the Marines aren't sure if Reckless will run away when she first experiences combat. What does Reckless do that convinces her Platoon that she's a brave and unusual horse?

Carefully look at the drawings that illustrate this story. In what ways do the drawings reflect war? In what ways do they show heroism?

The last sentence on page 29 reads, "Marines came from all over the country to honor the little red horse with the big heart." In this sentence, what does "big heart" mean? What would be a literal translation of this phrase?

ABOUT THE AUTHOR

Melissa Higgins writes fiction and nonfiction for children and young adults. Her nearly 30 nonfiction titles range from science and technology to history and biographies. While her wide array of topics reflects her varied interests, she especially enjoys writing about admirable behavior. She was drawn to Reckless' story because it proves animals can be heroic too. Before becoming a full-time writer, Ms. Higgins worked as a school counselor. When she's not writing, she enjoys hiking and taking photographs in the Arizona desert where she lives with her husband.

ABOUT THE ILLUSTRATOR

My name is Alvaro "Alva" Iglesias. I'm a strange guy who is always surrounded by cats, dogs, and pencils. I started drawing at age 6, and I still cannot stop. My work is mostly for comics, animation films, and illustration, although I have also done graphic design and tattoos.

I live and work in a old house in a small village near the forest in Cantabria, North of Spain. I live with my girlfriend, who is a veterinarian and keeps the house full of animals–it's great.

LOOK FOR ALL THE BOOKS IN THE ANIMAL HEROES SERIES:

Editor: Jeni Wittrock
Designer: Ashlee Suker
Art Director: Nathan Gassman
Production Specialist: Tori Abraham
The illustrations in this book were created digitally.

Picture Window Books are published by Capstone,
1710 Roe Crest Drive, North Mankato, Minnesota 56003
www.capstonepub.com

Library of Congress Cataloging-in-Publication Data
Higgins, Melissa, 1953–
Sgt. Reckless the War Horse: Korean War Hero/by Melissa Higgins; illustrated by Alvaro Iglesias.
pages cm.—(Nonfiction picture books. Animal Heroes)
Includes bibliographical references.
Summary: "Simple text and full-color illustrations describe the true story of Staff Sergeant Reckless, the Korean War horse"—Provided by publisher.
ISBN 978-1-4795-5462-1 (library binding)
ISBN 978-1-4795-5466-9 (paperback)
ISBN 978-1-4795-5760-8 (paper over board)
ISBN 978-1-4795-5470-6 (ebook pdf)
1. Sgt. Reckless (Horse)—Juvenile literature. 2. Korean War, 1950–1953—Participation, American—Juvenile literature. 3. War horses—United States—History—20th century. 4. United States. Marine Corps—History—Korean War, 1950-1953—Juvenile literature. I. Title. II. Title: Sergeant Reckless, the war horse.
DS919.H45 2015
951.904'2450929—dc23   2014011230

Photo Credit:
Marine Corps Archives & Special Collections, 29

Printed in the United States of America in
North Mankato, Minnesota
032014   008087CGF14

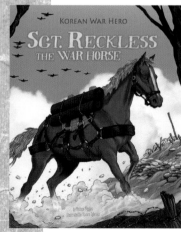

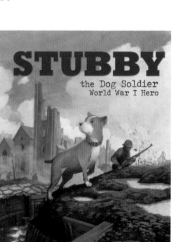